BLACKW
HABITAT FIELD
Flowering Plants of
Salt Marshes and Sand Dunes

Michael Quigley

*Senior Lecturer in Environmental Biology,
Nene College, Northampton*

Robin Crump

*Warden and Director of Studies,
Orielton Field Centre, Nr. Pembroke, Dyfed*

Basil Blackwell

Acknowledgements

I wish to express my thanks to all my colleagues at Nene College who have supported this venture. I should especially like to thank Jeffery Best who offered valuable advice in the construction and content of the keys. Our wives, Roz and Ann, we thank for their patience and encouragement during the preparation of this guide.

The cover photograph is by Brian Armson and shows sea holly.

Introduction

Salt marshes and sand dunes are excellent habitats in which to study plant zonation.

Coastal salt marshes are formed, within estuaries, from fine sediments brought on to mudflats by water transport. They develop in areas of sufficient shelter from tidal wave action to allow deposition of alluvial material. Terrestrial flowering plants specially adapted to soils of a high salt content (halophytes) begin to colonise the mudflats between tidal levels of mean high water of neap tides (MHWN) and mean high water (MHW). The establishment and subsequent development of certain primary colonising plants encourage further deposition and stabilisation of sediment. With time, continued deposition of sediments raises the marsh level with a consequent change in environmental conditions. Such changes are reflected in changes in the flora. This is seen in a changing zonation of plant communities on an established marsh. Such a dynamic zonation reflects the changes which occur with time, i.e. a succession. A comparable development occurs on certain sandy shores where coarse sediments (sand) are transported by wind. Sand dune formation is dependent upon adequate supplies of sand and sufficient wind.

In both habitats, vegetation plays two roles; it stabilises existing surfaces and speeds up further deposition of sediment material.

Quantitative investigations

In order to investigate effectively the distribution and abundance of plant species on salt marshes and sand dunes, certain quantitative techniques should be considered. Each individual plant of a particular species forms part of a population. Rarely is it possible to obtain information (data) for all populations or the whole of one population. It is more usual to rely on some data from samples and from these data to obtain a picture of the population (or populations) as a whole. It is important that information obtained from samples is representative of the population (populations) under consideration.

Sampling unit

Plant **cover** may be used as a method of providing information of distribution and abundance. Cover may be defined as the proportion of the ground occupied by the aerial parts of individual plants.

Estimation of cover requires the use of a sampling unit. A simple method is to use a square quadrat frame of 50 cm sides divided into 100 equal sub-units. Within such a frame, cover may be estimated by eye or a more precise estimate may be obtained by using a pointing technique. In this case a long pointing pin is held vertically in the top left-hand corner of each sub-unit. Each species touched by the pin is recorded. This is repeated for all 100 squares. The number of times that a particular species is recorded as touching a pin is a direct estimate of percentage cover. The percentage cover of the bare ground can also be estimated in this manner.

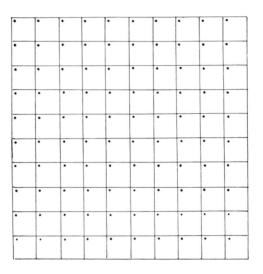

• indicates position of pointing pin

quadrat frame (50 cm sides)

Sampling method

The choice of sampling method will depend upon the nature of the investigation, the pattern and morphology of the plants and the time available.

Random sampling

This may be regarded as the 'ideal' method for, by definition, each sampling unit has an equal chance of being chosen within the designated sampling area. In order to achieve this, quadrats must be positioned with precision.

Decide upon the size of the sampling area and set out metre tapes or lines marked in 50 cm intervals to form a square. Locate the position for placing each quadrat by using pairs of random numbers (obtainable from statistical tables) as co-ordinates. This may be done prior to the sampling exercise. Arrange the pairs of co-ordinates in order (from the lowest to the highest pairs of numbers) to enable you to work through the sampling area systematically. You may use movable metre tapes, set at right angles, to locate each quadrat position. Place each quadrat to the right of the intersections of the co-ordinates.

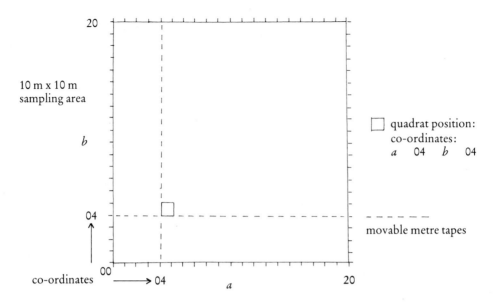

20

10 m x 10 m
sampling area

b

quadrat position:
co-ordinates:
a   04   b   04

04

movable metre tapes

co-ordinates   00   → 04   20

a

Inevitably you must decide upon the number of quadrats necessary to sample the population(s). As a general rule 'the more the better' applies. However, a guide to the minimum number can be obtained by plotting the running means against the number of quadrats. The minimum number is the number of quadrats that correspond to the point where oscillations level out. The final decision on the number of quadrats must be left to you; however, in practice we have found that 20 quadrats in each area will give a representative picture of plant cover.

Belt transects

These are a form of systematic sampling where quadrats are positioned linearly at right angles to any apparent zonation of plant communities.

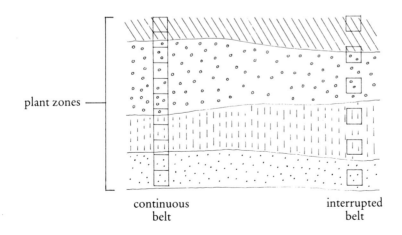

plant zones

continuous
belt

interrupted
belt

The decision on whether to employ a continuous or an interrupted belt transect is largely dependent upon the width of the apparent zones of plant communities. Belt transects should only be used where it is suspected that the conditions which influence plant distribution show a gradient of change.

Example: gradients of change in environmental factors

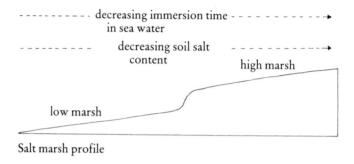

Salt marsh profile

Levelling technique

For belt transect exercises where changes in the topography of the ground exist, you may wish to prepare a profile of the area under investigation. This will require the use of a levelling technique. One such technique is described below.

Equipment

Two (2 m) ranging poles divided into centimetre sections (a centimetre tape can be attached)
One (2 m) bar divided into 0.5 m sections
One spirit-level

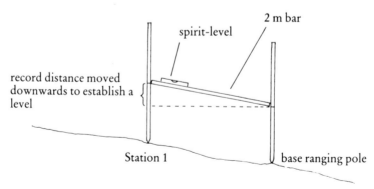

Procedure

1 Set up the equipment as indicated in the diagram above. Place each end of the 2 m bar (spirit-level attached) against the metre marks on the upright ranging poles. *Caution:* if the slope of the ground is such that a 2 m separation of the bar between the ranging poles is impossible, reduce the separation interval to 1 m. Record the interval on your data sheet.
2 Move the end of the 2 m bar at Station 1 upwards or downwards to establish a level (indicated with the spirit-level). Record the distance moved on the ranging pole in centimetres. If an upward movement is needed, record the value followed by a + sign, e.g. 10 cm+; if a downward movement, record the value followed by a − sign. Record the value on your data sheet.
3 Move the base ranging pole to the next position above Station 1 and repeat the procedure described until the levelling exercise is complete.

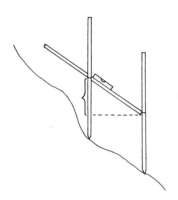

Levelling data sheet						
Recorder:		Location:			Date:	
A: Enter the number of the station and any change in levelling interval below 2 m.						
B: Record an upward movement of the bar as the value followed by + and a downward movement as the value followed by −.						
C: Record the accumulated total.						

A	B	C	A	B	C
2 m	10 cm+	10			
2 m	20 cm+	30			
2 m	10 cm−	20			

Investigations of plant zonation

Salt marshes

We suggest that for a preliminary investigation an interrupted belt transect technique be used. This may be coupled with a levelling exercise from the landward edge of the marsh to a suitable point on the upper marsh. You may achieve this in the following manner.

1 Select an appropriate transect line at right angles to the apparent zonation of plant communities. N.B. In order to avoid unnecessary damage to plants, minimise the trampling of plants.

2 Level along the transect line at regular 2 m intervals (reduce the interval to 1 m if necessary). Record the data.

3 At each levelling station, beginning at the base station, place a quadrat frame in such a way that its centre corresponds to the position of each ranging pole. Estimate the percentage cover of the plants and record all results.

Sand dunes

In order to obtain meaningful results from a preliminary investigation of dune system zonation of plant communities we suggest that a random sampling technique be used.

If at all possible, dune areas or zones of different age should be selected for analysis. Areas which correspond to embryo, early and late yellow and finally grey dunes should provide a picture of changes in plant communities. For this purpose, regard embryo dunes as the youngest zones, and grey dunes as the oldest zones.

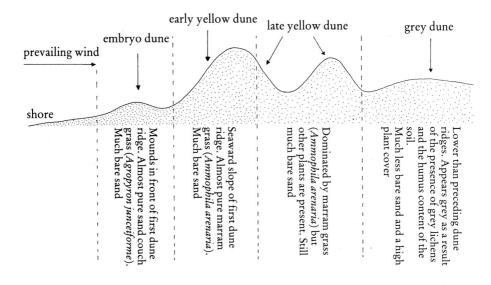

Within each zone, select a suitably sized sampling area and proceed to estimate plant cover as indicated on page 1. We have found a suitable sampling area to be a 10 m x 10 m square for each group of students if the results of two or more groups are subsequently amalgamated. N.B. If the time available for investigation is limited, you may wish to decide upon a maximum number of sampling units within each area. If this is the case and the group of students is large enough for a number of sampling areas to be considered, combine the results of percentage cover for each species for analysis purposes.

Presentation of data

Preparation of a profile diagram

Conventional centimetre and millimetre A4 graph paper is suitable for the preparation of a profile diagram and any data that you wish to include of plant distribution and abundance.

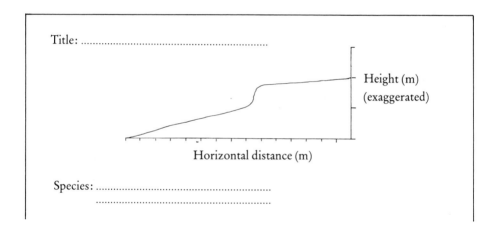

Use the accumulated total figures and the horizontal distance worked during the levelling exercise to produce the profile in the following manner.

1 The highest recorded number of the accumulated total will represent the maximum height of the profile. Convert this figure to metres, e.g. 375 cm = 3.75 m.

2 Determine the horizontal distance worked. Take into account any changes in the levelling interval.

3 Decide upon an appropriate exaggerated scale to represent the height data in relation to the horizontal distance worked (e.g. height scale is four times the horizontal scale). This is common practice and highlights any changes in topographical features.

4 Draw the vertical and horizontal axes on the graph paper.

5 Plot the accumulated total figures above the appropriate levelling stations along the horizontal axis as indicated below.

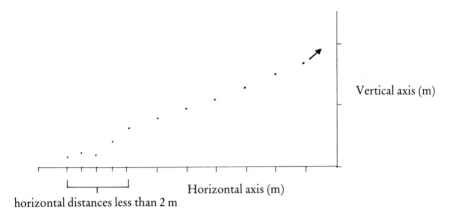

horizontal distances less than 2 m

6 Join up the points to produce the profile.

Analysis of vegetation based on percentage cover

Salt marshes

The percentage cover data for each plant species recorded may be plotted below a profile of the marsh as vertical bar graphs. Each bar graph should correspond to an appropriate levelling station on the profile. Draw bars of 2 mm width and let 1 mm in height represent 5% cover (2 cm will, therefore, represent 100% cover). Allow sufficient space between each plant species to avoid any overlap.

You may follow the plan illustrated below.

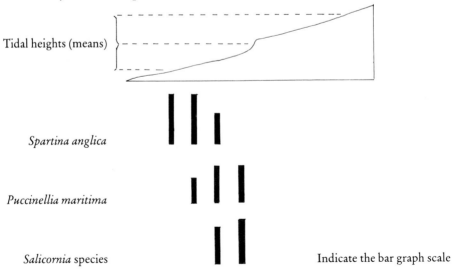

Sand dunes

Plot the data of percentage cover for sand and plant species for each of the dune zones considered. You may use conventional centimetre and millimetre A4 graph paper for this purpose. Begin with the embryo dunes and finish with the grey dunes. Use bar graphs of 1 cm width and allow 1 cm in height to represent 20% cover for each species.

You may follow the plan illustrated below.

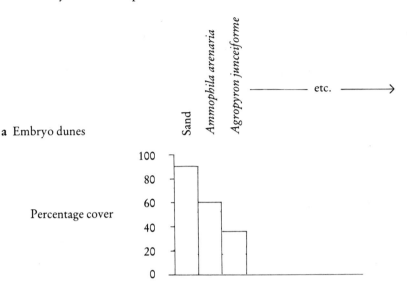

a Embryo dunes

b Early yellow dunes
c Late yellow dunes
d Grey dunes

An Introduction to the Habitat Keys

The series of selected habitat keys for flowering plants has been designed for the beginner in field studies and any other interested person. It is hoped that the keys will provide a straightforward method of identifying the more common flowering plants which occur in the habitats considered.

There is inevitably a flaw in this approach that the user should bear in mind. Since only the more commonly occurring plants are included, it is possible that you will encounter plants which are not mentioned in the keys. It is important that you do not attempt to make a particular plant fit one of the descriptions given. Should you wish to identify plants not considered in the keys, it is suggested that you refer to the bibliography for suitable references. For most purposes *The Wild Flower Key* by Francis Rose is highly recommended.

How to use the keys

Before you attempt to identify a plant, familiarise yourself with the lay-out of the keys. Scientific and common names are given for all the plants considered in each key. Line diagrams are also provided in the hope that they will support the written descriptions. Do not rely on the diagrams alone to identify the plant. Use the glossary provided to obtain descriptions of terms used in the keys which are unfamiliar to you.

Always work through the key in a systematic manner using the instructions given below. Do not attempt to make a plant fit a particular description. The plant in question may not be in the keys.

1 On the left-hand side of each page are numbers arranged in sequence with numbers in brackets beside them. The numbers in brackets will enable you to retrace your identification if you feel that you have made a mistake. Each number is set against a pair of contrasting statements **a** and **b**. (In some cases, three statements **a**, **b** and **c** are given.) One of these statements should provide a partial description of the plant which you wish to identify. Examine each plant carefully, using a 10x hand lens where necessary to provide details of the structure. Then study each statement and decide which most closely describes your specimen.

2 Each statement ends *either* in an arrow pointing to a number *or* in a box naming a plant. If the statement ends in an arrow, this means 'go on to' the number indicated. Find this number on the left-hand side of a page and continue your identification until a statement ends by naming a plant. At this point the identification is complete.

Glossary

achene	a small nut-like fruit
acute	a sharp angle, less than a right-angle
alternate	leaves alternating up the stem — first on one side and then on the other
anther	see **flower**
awn	a stiff, bristle-like projection arising from the spikelets of grasses
axis	main stem running through an inflorescence

alternate

awn

basal	leaves at the base of the stem at ground level
bract	a leaf with a flower in its axil
bracteole	a tiny leaf on a flower-stem without a flower in its axil
bristle-like (leaves)	tightly rolled and appearing like a bristle

bract

calyx	see **flower**
capsule	dry fruit that opens into two or more parts or by a lid or holes to release seeds
catkin	a spike of minute flowers, male and female borne separately
compound	a leaf divided into distinct, separate leaflets

—catkin

trifoliate   palmate   1-pinnate   2-pinnate   3-pinnate

converging	tendency to meet at a point
corolla	see **flower**
corymb	an inflorescence with the outer flower-stalks much longer than the inner ones. The flowers are at roughly the same level in a flat-topped cluster
cyme	an inflorescence in which the top flowers open first. Lower flowers open in sequence lowest opening last
deciduous	a woody plant which loses its leaves in the autumn
disc	see **florets**
diverging	tendency to spread from a point

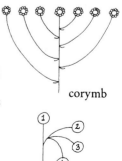
corymb

cyme

elliptical (leaves)	see diagram
entire (leaves)	a leaf without teeth or other indentations along its edge
evergreen	a woody plant which retains a covering of leaves throughout the year

elliptical

florets (disc and ray)	small flowers especially in the flower-head of plants of the daisy, dandelion and thistle families

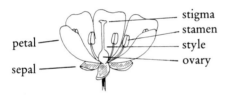

ray florets

disc florets

flower	the sexual reproductive organs of flowering plants. They are very varied in form and arrangement

stigma
stamen
petal
style
sepal
ovary

calyx	the outermost whorl composed of a number of leaf-like **sepals**. Sepals may be fused to form a **calyx tube**
corolla	next whorl within the calyx composed of usually coloured **petals**. Petals may be fused to form a **corolla tube**
stamens	a whorl or whorls of the male reproductive organs within the corolla. Each stamen is normally divided into a stalk or **filament** and a head or **anther**
carpel(s)	the innermost part of the flower divided into **ovary, style** and **stigma**
fruit	dry or fleshy outer case surrounding the seed of a plant
halberd-shaped (leaves)	like a medieval spearhead
indented (leaf margin)	
inflated	distended, swollen

halberd-shaped

inflorescence	flowering branch. Any grouping of flowers on a stem or in leaf-axils	
lanceolate (leaves)	lance-shaped	lanceolate
leaflets	the separate leaf-blades of a compound leaf	
ligule(s) (in grasses)	a small flap of tissue or fringe of hairs where the leaf-blade joins its sheathing base	
linear (leaves)	long, narrow, more or less parallel-sided leaf	
lyre shaped (leaves)	see diagram	

lyre-shaped

ligule   leaf-blade

membranous (ligules)	a flap of tissue	
midrib	the main, central vein of a leaf	
oblong (leaves)	a leaf about two or three times as long as broad, parallel sided in the central part	
opposite (leaves)	leaves arising in pairs	
oval, ovate (leaves)	rather egg shaped, about twice as long as broad	

oblong   oval

opposite

palmate	see **compound**
panicle	a branched raceme (see **raceme**)
pendulous	hanging down
pinnate (1, 2 or 3)	see **compound**
pinnatifid (leaves)	a deeply cut leaf but not cut right to midrib
prickles	a sharp, usually curved, outgrowth from the outer layers
prostrate	lying in a horizontal position

pinnatifid

raceme	a more or less elongated inflorescence in which the lowest flower opens first, and then the others open in sequence towards the tip
rhizome	a creeping, underground stem
root-leaves	leaves arranged at the stem base at ground level

raceme   panicle

13

rosette (of leaves)	leaves arranged in a more or less flat position to the ground
runner	a creeping stem above the ground, can root at tip to form a new plant

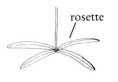

rosette

sepals	see **flower**
sessile	without a stalk
sheath	lower part of the leaf surrounding a stem
shrub	a woody plant without a main trunk, branched from the base
simple (leaves)	not divided into leaflets, margin may be entire, lobed or toothed
spike	an unbranched flower-head
spikelet	unit of a grass flower-head
spike-like	resembling a spike
spine	a stiff straight sharp-pointed structure
spur (in flowers)	a cylindrical or conical, sometimes curved, hollow projection from the back of certain flowers
stamens	see **flower**
stigma	see **flower**
stipules	leaf-like or scale-like structures at the base of the leaf-stalk or stem
stolon	a creeping stem above ground, not necessarily rooting at tip
strap-shaped	flat, parallel-sided, blunt-tipped leaf

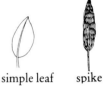

simple leaf   spike

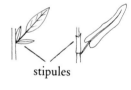

spikelets

stipules

terminal	at the tip
thorn	a woody sharp-pointed structure
tree	a woody plant with a main trunk
trifoliate	see **compound**
tufted	loose, compact or dense cluster
tussock	a clump

umbel	a flat-topped inflorescence with several branches all arising from one point at the top of the main stem, may be simple or compound
umbel-like	like an umbel inflorescence

umbel

whorl	more than two structures (e.g. leaves) of the same kind arising at the same level

whorl

The Common Flowering Plants of Salt Marshes

Use the information given below to determine the group to which your plant belongs and proceed to the section indicated by one of the letters A, B, C, D or E. (Use the glossary if you do not understand any of the terms used in the key.)

1   Leaves **reduced to triangular lobes**, main stem and branches jointed into **swollen sausage-like segments**. Plant dark, shining green to grey – green or yellow, often tinged red or purple.

> *Salicornia* species
> Glassworts

2   Leaves simple, margins entire, long narrow-linear and fleshy (succulent).

> SECTION A
> Page 16

3   Leaves simple, margins entire, long narrow-linear, grass-like or cylindrical, not fleshy (succulent). Flowers small, usually clustered, individually inconspicuous (in some plants the leaves may be reduced to scales at the base of the plant).

> SECTION B
> Pages 16–19

4   Leaves simple, margins entire, long oval or lanceolate, fleshy (succulent), mealy or leathery.

> SECTION C
> Page 20

5   Leaves simple of various shapes but not as above, most fleshy (succulent).

> SECTION D
> Pages 21–22

6   Leaves divided (pinnatifid) or compound (divided into distinct leaflets).

> SECTION E
> Page 23

SECTION A

inflorescence

1 a Leaves **half-cylindrical** with bases sheathing stems. Plant 15–50 cm tall, **without a woody rootstock**. Inflorescence spike-like with globular individual flowers on short stalks.

Triglochin maritima Sea Arrowgrass

sheathing base

  b Plant **with a woody rootstock**. —————————————▶ 2

2 a Leaves in rosettes. Plant cushion-forming, leaves **one-veined, round** in section, 2–20 cm long. Inflorescence stalks 5–30 cm tall, more or less downy, bearing terminal rounded heads of pink or white five-petalled flowers. A brown sleeve-like sheath extends down the stem from the base of the flower.

Armeria maritima Thrift

  b Leaves **three- to five-veined** in basal rosettes but standing in a more or less upright position, 5–20 cm long. Inflorescence stalks erect, unfurrowed with an inflorescence spike (2–6 cm long) at the tip. Flowers very closely arranged, corollas brown, stamens yellow.

Plantago maritima Sea Plantain

SECTION B

1 a Leaves **narrow-linear** in two vertical ranks. Stems **hollow and round**. —————————▶ 2 | Grasses |

  b Leaves **long linear** in three vertical ranks. Stems **solid**, often three-angled, sometimes rounded. —————————————————————▶ 8 | Sedges |

  c Leaves **cylindrical** or **grass-like**, hairless, sometimes reduced to scales. Stems may be three-angled in part. —————————————————————▶ 9 | Rushes |

16

2 (1) **a** Ligules **densely silky hairy**. Leaf-blades firm with a fine point. Inflorescences stiff **spike**. Spikelets narrowly oblong and flattened, closely overlapping in two rows and flattened on either side of the axis. Grass 30–130 cm tall, forming clumps and extensive meadows low on the marsh.

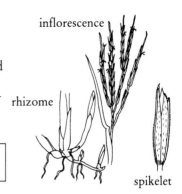

inflorescence

rhizome

spikelet

Spartina anglica
Common Cord Grass

b Ligules **membranous**, may be inconspicuous. ⟶ 3

3 (2) **a** Grass with creeping surface stolons. Leaf-blades slender, folded or inrolled, 2–20 cm long, greyish-green, blunt or abruptly pointed. Inflorescences stiff, linear. Spikelets narrowly oblong, 5–13 mm long. Grass to 80 cm tall, densely tufted, found low on the marsh, usually zoned above *Spartina anglica*.

inflorescence

spikelet

Puccinellia maritima
Common Salt-marsh Grass

b Stolons absent but underground rhizomes may be present. ⟶ 4

4 (3) **a** Leaves **bristle-like**. Inflorescence branched. Ligules inconspicuous.
⟶ 5

b Leaves **not bristle-like**. ⟶ 6

5 (4) **a** Grass 15–90 cm tall, **with slender short creeping rhizomes**. Leaf sheath **a closed tube** round stems. Leaf-blades bluish-green.

Festuca rubra
Red Fescue

b Grass 5–60 cm tall, **without rhizomes**. Leaf sheath a tube round the stem, **split at least half-way down**. Plant densely tufted.

Festuca ovina
Sheep's Fescue

6 (4) **a** Grass **with wiry rhizomes.** Leaf-blades **sharply pointed** with **hard tips,** 8–35 cm long, flat or tightly inrolled, stiff. Inflorescences spike-like **stiff.** Spikelets **closely overlapping and alternating** in two rows on opposite sides of the axis. Grass 20–120 cm tall, forming tufts or large patches.

> *Agropyron pungens*
> Sea Couch

spikelet

inflorescence

b Grass **without rhizomes.** Inflorescences spike-like. ⟶ ▶ 7

7 (6) **a** Leaf-blades bluish-green, **flat,** 1.5–8 cm long. Spike stiff, dense, spikelets **with long extending awns.** Grass 10–40 cm tall.

> *Hordeum marinum*
> Sea Barley

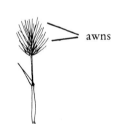

awns

b Leaf-blades greyish-green, **Hairless,** pointed, 1–6 cm long, flat or inrolled. Spikes with **spikelets embedded in hollows in spike axis.** Grass up to 40 cm tall.

> *Parapholis strigosa*
> Sea Hard Grass

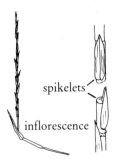

spikelets

inflorescence

8 (1) **a** Stems **sharply angled**, 30–100 cm tall, rough towards the top. Leaves **keeled**, to 10 mm wide, margins rough. Inflorescence spikes dark brown, narrowly egg-shaped, sometimes a cluster, overtopped by a long **narrow leaf-like** bract.

Scirpus maritimus   Sea Club Rush

b Stems **three-angled, smooth, almost leafless.** Plant 20–40 cm tall, rather stiff. Leaves greyish, narrow, grooved. Sheaths blackish. Inflorescence spikes unstalked with one male and two to three short fat females, very long **spreading** bracts.

Carex extensa   Salt-marsh Sedge

9 (1) **a** Plant **tufted, with rhizomes, forming extensive patches.** Leaves dark green, mostly from the lower part of the stem. Inflorescence stems 10–50 cm tall, **curved, flattened below, three-angled above.** Inflorescences with **dark brown** flowers in a loose cluster, usually overtopping the leaf-like bracts.

Juncus gerardii   Mud Rush

b Plant **erect, tough, densely tufted**, stem 30–100 cm tall, **light green,** smooth when fresh. Leaves only near the base, flat, sharp-pointed. Inflorescences of **yellow** flowers in a large loose cluster with ascending branches near the top of the stem.

Juncus maritimus   Sea Rush

SECTION C

1 a Leaves **leathery**, in basal rosettes, stalked, with a curved spine at the tips, elliptical-lanceolate, 4–12 cm long. Plant 8–40 cm tall. Inflorescence rounded or flat-topped branched panicle bearing lilac–blue **papery** flowers.

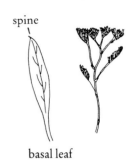

spine

basal leaf

| *Limonium* species |
| Sea Lavenders |

b Leaves **fleshy** or **mealy**, not restricted to a basal rosette. ——————▶ 2

2 a Plant with **fleshy basal** and **alternate** long-oval or oblong-linear **stem**-leaves, erect, 15–100 cm tall, hairless. Leaves 7–12 cm long. Basal leaves stalked. Flower-heads daisy-like in loose umbel-like corymbs, outer florets mauve, inner disc florets yellow.

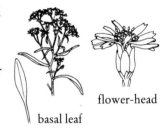

flower-head

basal leaf

| *Aster tripolium* |
| Sea Aster |

b Plant **low shrub** to 80 cm tall, sprawling. Lower leaves **elliptical, stalked, opposite, whitish mealy**. Upper leaves narrower. Inflorescences of dense spikes of tiny greyish-yellow flowers.

inflorescence

| *Halimione portulacoides* |
| Sea Purslane |

1   a Leaves **fleshy with papery stipules** at leaf bases. ————▶ 2

      b Leaves **without stipules** at leaf bases. ————▶ 3

2 (1) a Plant creeping to ascending, up to **30 cm** long. Leaves **pointed, flat above, rounded below**, 1–2.5 cm long, **opposite**. Flowers **white or pink**, 6–8 mm across, five-petalled, ten stamens.

> *Spergularia media*
> Greater Sea Spurrey

      b Similar to **a** but only up to **20 cm** long. Flowers **deep pink**, 6–8 mm across, four to eight or fewer stamens.

> *Spergularia marina*
> Lesser Sea Spurrey

3 (1) a Leaves **opposite, oval-pointed**, stalkless, 4–12 mm long. Plant creeping and ascending, 10–30 cm long. Flowers solitary, in leaf-axils, 5 mm across with pink five-lobed calyx, five stamens.

> *Glaux maritima*
> Sea Milkwort

flower

      b Leaves **alternate**. ————▶ 4

4   a Leaves **fleshy** and rather **sausage-shaped**. ————▶ 5

      b Leaves **fleshy** but **of other shape**. ————▶ 6

5 (4) a Leaves 3–25 mm long, **half-cylindrical**, tapered to base, green, often red-flushed. Plant branched, prostrate to erect, up to 60 cm tall. Flowers 1–2 mm across, in small clusters with five fleshy sepals, no petals and five stamens.

> *Suaeda maritima*
> Annual Sea Blite

close-up of flowers and leaves

      b Similar to **a** but **shrubby**, 60–120 cm tall. Leaves **cylindrical**. Southeast England from Dorset to Lincolnshire.

> *Suaeda fruticosa*
> Shrubby Sea Blite

6 (4) **a** Stem-leaves **spoon-** or **heart**-shaped, clasping. Basal leaves **kidney-** or **heart-shaped**, stalked. Plant with one or more ascending stems, 5–50 cm long. Flowers with four white petals, rarely lilac.

> *Cochlearia officinalis*
> Common Scurvygrass

basal leaf

b Similar to **a** but basal leaves with **wedge-shaped** bases tapering into stalks.

> *Cochlearia anglica*
> English Scurvygrass

basal leaf

c Leaves **triangular** or **diamond-shaped**. Flowers angled, green. ————————————————➤ **7**

7 (6) **a** Lower leaves **triangular**, 3–6 cm long, the leaf base making a right-angle with the stalk. Flowers in terminal and leaf-axil spikes.

> *Atriplex hastata*
> Hastate Orache

leaf

b Similar to **a** but lower leaves **diamond-shaped** with the leaf base tapering gradually into a stalk.

> *Atriplex patula*
> Common Orache

leaves

SECTION E

1 a Leaves **lobed, toothed** or **pinnatifid**, one-veined, 2–6 cm long, in **basal rosette**. Plant usually downy. Inflorescence spike of closely set flowers with brownish corollas and yellow stamens.

leaves

> *Plantago coronopus*
> Buck's-horn Plantain

b Leaves **compound.** ─────────────────────────➤ 2

2 a Leaves 2–5 cm long, two-pinnate, segments linear, blunt, lower stalked, **all white woolly** both sides. Plant strongly aromatic, 20–50 cm tall. Flower-heads many oval, in panicles, florets yellow or reddish.

> *Artemesia maritima*
> Sea Wormwood

b Stem- and root-leaves two-pinnate. Root leaves with narrow, bluntly pointed elliptical leaflets without teeth (soon withering). Stem-leaves with narrow-linear pointed leaflets. Plant 30–100 cm tall. Flowers small in open umbels.

leaf

> *Oenanthe lachenalii*
> Parsley Water-dropwort

Some Common Flowering Plants of Sand Dunes

The guide to flowering plants of aquatic habitats may be useful if you wish to identify species from wet areas between dunes (dune slacks). Use the information given below to determine the group to which your plant belongs and proceed to the section indicated by one of the letters A, B, C, D, E or F. (Use the glossary if you do not understand any of the terms used in the key.)

1   Leaves linear, margins entire, grass-like. Flowers small, usually clustered, individually inconspicuous.

> SECTION A
> Pages 25–27

2   Woody shrubs and/or plants with thorns, prickles or spines.

> SECTION B
> Pages 27–29

3   Herbaceous plants with leaves in **basal rosettes only**. Leaf margins entire, toothed or lobed.

> SECTION C
> Pages 30–31

4   Herbaceous plants with **fleshy** (succulent) leaves. Leaf margin entire or variously cut.

> SECTION D
> Pages 32–34

5   Herbaceous plants with **simple leaves, not fleshy**. Margins of leaves entire or toothed, variously arranged.

> SECTION E
> Pages 34–39

6   Herbaceous plants which are **not fleshy**. Leaves **deeply lobed** or **pinnatifid** or **compound**.

> SECTION F
> Pages 40–41

1   a Leaves long-linear, in **three** vertical ranks, coarse, 1.5–5 mm wide. Stem **solid, three-angled**. Flowers five to twelve in a crowded spike. Plant often rabbit grazed and appears chewed.

> *Carex arenaria*
> Sand Sedge

     b Leaves long-linear, in **two** vertical ranks. Stems **hollow** and **round**. ➤ 2

2 (1) a Leaves **tightly inrolled, bristle-like**. Ligules very small. Inflorescences branched. ➤ 3

     b Leaves **not bristle-like** but **may be inrolled**. Inflorescences **spike-like**. ➤ 4

3 (2) a Grass 15–90 cm tall, **with slender short creeping rhizomes**. Leaf sheath a **closed** tube round the stem. Leaf-blades bluish-green.

> *Festuca rubra* (var. *arenaria*)
> Red Fescue

     b Grass 5–60 cm tall, **without rhizomes**. Leaf sheath a tube round the stem **split at least half-way down**. Plant densely tufted.

> *Festuca ovina*
> Sheep's Fescue

4 (2) a Leaf-blades usually 20 cm or more in length. **Large grasses spreading by rhizomes**. ➤ 5

     b Leaf-blades **short** (often less than 10 cm). **Small grasses not spreading by rhizomes**. ➤ 7

5 (4) **a** Ligule **a long stiff spike** (to 3 cm long), often splitting. Plant 50–120 cm tall, spreading extensively by stout rhizomes. Leaf-blades greyish-green, sharp-pointed, to 60 cm long. Inflorescences narrowly oblong to lanceolate-oblong, 7–22 cm long. Spikelets closely overlapping.

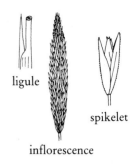

ligule

spikelet

inflorescence

| *Ammophila arenaria* |
| Marram Grass |

b Ligules **inconspicuous.** ⟶ 6

6 (5) **a** Plant 20–60 cm tall, forming loose tufts or mats, spreading by long **wiry rhizomes.** Leaf-blades finely pointed, up to 35 cm long, usually **drooping.** Inflorescences 4–20 cm long. Spikelets **alternating in two rows on opposite sides of the axis, easily breaking.** On embryo dunes and fore-dunes.

inflorescence

spikelet

| *Agropyron junceiforme* |
| Sand Couch |

b Plant 60–200 cm tall, forming large tufts or masses, with long **stout rhizomes.** Leaf-blades sharply pointed, up to 60 cm long, **rigid.** Inflorescences compact, stiff, 15–35 cm long. Spikelets **in pairs alternating on two opposite sides of the axis, oblong or wedge-shaped, not easily breaking.**

spikelet

inflorescence

| *Elymus arenarius* |
| Lyme Grass |

7 (4) **a** Ligules **inconspicuous**. Spikelets **with long awns**. Plant 10–60 cm tall. Leaf-blades blunt-tipped, 1–10 cm long, may be inrolled, up to 3 mm wide, with **prominent ribs**. Inflorescences stiff, narrowly oblong, 2–12 cm long. Spikelets **closely overlapping**.

inflorescence

spikelet

awns

> *Vulpia* species
> Sand Fescue

b Ligules **membranous**. Spikelets **without obvious awns**. ——▶ 8

8 (7) **a** Ligules up to 7 mm long. Plant 1–15 cm (but can be up to 30 cm) tall, tufted or solitary. Leaf-blades whitish-green or pale green, narrowed to a fine point, 0.5–6 cm long, **flat**. Inflorescences **narrowly cylindrical, rounded at the tip**. Spikelets **densely crowded**, pale or whitish-green, sometimes tinged purple.

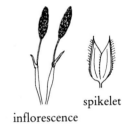

inflorescence

spikelet

> *Phleum arenarium*
> Sand Cat's-tail

b Ligules 0.5–3 mm long. Plant 3–20 cm tall. Leaf-blades 1–10 cm long, narrowing to a fine blunt tip, dark green. Inflorescences **narrow**, 0.5–7 cm long. Spikelets **rigid in two rows on one side of axis**.

inflorescence

spikelet

> *Catapodium marinum*
> Stiff Sand-grass

SECTION B

1 **a** Plant **with thorns, prickles or spines**. ——————————▶ 2

b Plant **without thorns, prickles or spines**. Leaves **opposite**. ——▶ 7

2 (1) **a** Plant with **long woody thorns.** Leaves simple, linear-lanceolate with **silvery scales, alternate,** up to 8 cm long, stalkless. Shrub to 3 m tall, densely branched. Flowers very small on short spikes in leaf-axils. Fruits orange berries.

> *Hippophae rhamnoides*
> Sea Buckthorn

b Plant with **prickles** or **spines.** ⸻▶ 3

3 (2) **a** **'Rose-like' prickles** on stems and leaves. ⸻▶ 4

b **Spines** present on leaves and stems or on leaves alone. ⸻▶ 5

4 (3) **a** **Many long straight prickles and long stiff bristles.** Plant low, patch-forming, to 50 cm tall. Leaves compound of three to five pairs of **toothed** leaflets, often **purple-flushed.** Flowers 'rose-like', solitary, five-petalled, cream, 20–40 mm across.

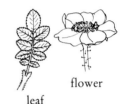

leaf flower

> *Rosa pimpinellifolia*
> Burnet Rose

b **Prickles curved.** Plant **scrambling,** erect or creeping shrubs. Leaves compound of three to five (or more) **pinnately** or **palmately** arranged. Flowers 'rose-like' with five cream petals and many stamens. Fruits 'blackberry-like'.

> *Rubus* species
> Brambles

5 (3) **a** **'Thistle-like' spines** on **leaves and stems.** Leaves oblong-lanceolate, **clasping** stem, wavy-lobed, **cottony below,** fringed with weak spines. Plant 10–60 cm tall, more or less **cottony** and **purple-flushed.** Flower-heads solitary or clustered, 3–4 cm across when open, 'thistle-like', **straw yellow ray flowers, brownish disc florets.**

> *Carlina vulgaris*
> Carline Thistle

b Spines on **leaves only.** ⸻▶ 6

6 (5) **a** Leaves **'holly-like' with long spines on margins.**
Stem-leaves stalkless, **waxy-grey with thick
margins.** Root-leaves long-stalked,
palmate-veined, rounded. Plant branched, 30–60
cm tall. Flowers **like 'teasle-heads'** in umbels,
bright clear blue.

> *Eryngium maritimum*
> Sea Holly

b Leaves **rounded and tapering into a spine.** Plant
fleshy, more or less prostrate, 20–40 cm long,
striped pale green or reddish, branched. Leaves
1–4 cm long. Flowers **tiny**, in leaf-axils. Drift line.

> *Salsola kali*
> Saltwort

7 (1) **a** Leaves **compound, leaflets narrow-oval, pointed.**
Plant a woody climber with peeling fibrous bark.
Flowers 2 cm across, terminal, in panicles in leaf-
axils, four greenish-creamy sepals, many stamens.
Fruits with long white plumed styles.

> *Clematis vitalba*
> Traveller's Joy

b Leaves **simple, elliptical-lanceolate**, 3–6 cm long.
Plant privet-like, semi-evergreen up to 5 m tall.
Flowers in terminal panicles, corolla white, 4–5
mm across, four-lobed, two stamens. Fruits black
shiny berries.

> *Ligustrum vulgare*
> Wild Privet

SECTION C

1   **a**   Leaf margins **entire**. Flowers 'dandelion-like'. Leaves 3–8 cm long with **stiff white hairs above, white-felted below**. Plant with long leafy runners. Flower-stems 5–30 cm tall. Flower-heads solitary of pale yellow florets.

> *Pilosella officinarum*
> Mouse-ear Hawkweed

     b   Leaf margins **entire** or **scarcely toothed**. Leaves **lanceolate** or **oval-lanceolate**, spreading or erect, with three to five strong, more or less parallel veins. Inflorescence stalk **deeply furrowed, silky hairy**, 10–40 cm long, oblong with many small flowers.

inflorescence

> *Plantago lanceolata*
> Ribwort Plantain

     c   Leaf margins **lobed, toothed** or **deeply cut**, without the combined features of **b**. ⟶ 2

2   (1) **a**   Leaves **fleshy** (succulent) **lobed, toothed** or **deeply cut**, one-veined, 2–6 cm long. Plant usually downy. Inflorescence a spike of closely set flowers with brownish corollas and yellow stamens.

leaves

> *Plantago coronopus*
> Buck's-horn Plantain

     b   Leaves **toothed, broad-lanceolate**, narrowed to **base**. Flowers **in short racemes**. Plant 2–10 cm tall (rarely more). Flower-stems leafless. Flowers white with four, deeply notched petals. Fruits oval to elliptical, flattened.

> *Erophila verna*
> Common Whitlowgrass

     c   Leaves **deeply cut** or **wavy-toothed**. Flowers 'dandelion-like'. ⟶ 3

3 (2) **a** Leaves **lanceolate**, margins **deeply cut**, sparsely hairy, lobes toothed, **directed backwards**. Flower-stems hollow **exuding a white milky juice** (when cut). Flower-heads solitary 2–6 cm across, florets bright yellow.

leaf

> *Taraxacum officinale*
> aggregate
> Dandelions – contains many
> similar microspecies

Taraxacum laevigatum may commonly occur on dunes. The plant is often small with narrow, deeply cut leaves.

leaf

b Leaves **wavy-toothed, hairy.** ──────────▶ 4

4 (3) **a** Leaves **with forked hairs.** ──────────▶ 5

b Leaves **hairy but hairs not forked, oblong–lanceolate**, 5–12 cm long, **bristly**. Flower-stems 20–40 cm tall, simple or branched **with a few scale-like bracts** along the stem. Flower-heads 2–4 cm across of bright yellow florets, **outer greyish beneath**.

leaf

> *Hypochaeris radicata*
> Common Cat's-ear

5 (4) **a** Leaves **lanceolate, coarse, narrowed at base**. Flower-stems leafless, 10–40 cm tall, unbranched. **Forked hairs throughout**. Florets golden-yellow, **outer usually orange** or **reddish beneath**.

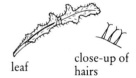
leaf   close-up of hairs

> *Leontodon hispidus*
> Rough Hawkbit

b Resembles **a** but flower-stems shorter, 8–12 cm tall. **Bristly below, hairless above**. Outer florets **grey-violet beneath**.

> *Leontodon taraxacoides*
> Hairy Hawkbit

SECTION D

1   **a** Leaves **kidney-** or **heart-shaped**. Plant creeping, hairless. Flower corollas trumpet-shaped, 25–40 mm across, pink with white stripes.

> *Calystegia soldanella*
> Sea Bindweed

    b Leaves **of other shape.** ────────────────► 2

2 (1) **a** Leaves **egg-shaped**, 3–5 mm long, yellow–green, may be red-flushed. Plant low, 2–10 cm long, **mat-forming**. Inflorescences branched. Flowers to 12 mm across, **star-shaped**, with five yellow petals.

flower

> *Sedum acre*
> Biting Stonecrop

    b Leaves **of other shape.** ────────────────► 3

3 (2) **a** Leaf margins **entire.** ────────────────► 4
    b Leaf margins **toothed** or **deeply lobed.** ──────────► 6

4 (3) **a** Leaves **opposite, sessile, oval, pointed**, 6–18 mm long, margins **wavy, translucent**. Plant creeping, flowering stems 5–25 cm tall. Flowers 6–10 mm across, **star-like**, five-petalled, greenish-white.

> *Honkenya peploides*
> Sea Sandwort

    b Leaves **alternate** or **spirally** arranged, close set on stems. ──────► 5

5 (4) **a** Leaves 0.5–2 cm long, **very thick, waxy-green, oval, blunt, midrib obscure**. Plant 20–40 cm tall with several erect stems, **exudes white milky juice** (when cut). Flowers **cup-shaped**, green, in open umbel-like heads. In **young** dune areas.

inflorescence

> *Euphorbia paralias*
> Sea Spurge

b Similar to **a** but more slender. Leaves rather **thinner** and **leathery, broadest above middle, tips pointed, midrib prominent below**. On **older** parts of dunes.

> *Euphorbia portlandica*
> Portland Spurge

6 (3) **a** Leaves **deeply lobed** (may be **pinnatifid**). ──────────▶ 7

    b Leaves **diamond, triangular** or **linear** in shape. ──────────▶ 8

7 (6) **a** Plant **cabbagy**, 40–60 cm tall, up to 100 cm across. Basal leaves **oval, long-stalked, waxy-grey**, hairless, up to 30 cm long with lobed, wavy-margins. Upper leaves **smaller and narrower**. Flowers white, four-petalled, 10–16 mm across in large flat-topped much-branched heads.

inflorescence

> *Crambe maritima*
> Sea Kale

leaf

b Lower leaves **narrowed into stalk**, more or less deeply pinnatifid, lobes oblong. Upper leaves **sessile, lobed** or **entire**. Plant sprawling and rising, 25–45 cm long. Flowers four-petalled, lilac-pink or white, in racemes.

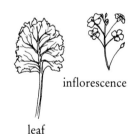

> *Cakile maritima*
> Sea Rocket

8 (6) **a** Lower leaves **triangular**, 3–6 cm long, leaf base making a **near right-angle with its stalk**. Plant prostrate to erect, 10–60 cm. Flowers green, spiky in spikes.

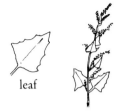

leaf

> *Atriplex hastata*
> Hastate Orache

b Plant similar to **a** but lower leaves **diamond-shaped** with leaf base **tapering gradually** into the stalk. Upper leaves **oblong-linear.**

leaves

> *Atriplex patula*
> Common Orache

c Plant differs from **a** and **b** in that **all leaves** are **linear** or **oblong-linear**. Plant erect, 50–100 cm tall.

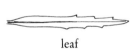

leaf

> *Atriplex littoralis*
> Grass-leaved Orache

SECTION E

1   **a** Leaves with **angular** or **tubular stipules** at bases. ⟶ 2

     b Leaves **without stipules** at bases. ⟶ 3

2 (1) **a** Leaves **oval**, toothed with **angular** stipules on leaf-stalks, **all stickily hairy** (sand sticks to them). Plant creeping and ascending, 30–60 cm long, up to 30 cm tall. **Hairy all round**. Flowers 'pea-like' **pink**.

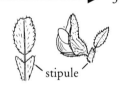

stipule

> *Ononis repens*
> Restharrow

b Stipules **tubular** on stems above leaf bases. Plant **'dock-like'**, hairless, 30–80 cm tall. Leaves shiny, **arrow-shaped**, up to 10 cm long, stalked below, stalkless and clasping above. Inflorescence branched with loose whorls of small **reddish** flowers.

> *Rumex acetosa*
> Common Sorrel

3 (1) **a** Leaves **in whorls.** ━━━━━━━━━━━━━━▶ 4

    b Leaves **alternate** (or **spirally arranged**). ━━━━━▶ 5

    c Leaves **opposite.** ━━━━━━━━━━━━━━━▶ 8

4 (3) **a** Leaves **linear, six** (or more) in a whorl. Stem-leaves creeping at base. Flower-stems more or less erect and **four-angled.** Flowers in leafy panicles, terminal, corollas 2–3 mm across, **golden-yellow** with pointed lobes.

> *Galium verum*
> Lady's Bedstraw

    b Leaves **four** in a whorl, 6–20 mm long, **often unequal** and at an **acute angle** to the stems. Plant hairless, prostrate, with branched **four-angled** ascending shoots, 5–20 cm tall. Inflorescence few-flowered, long-stalked, clustered, corollas funnel-shaped, **white inside, pink outside,** four-lobed.

inflorescence

> *Asperula cynanchica*
> Squinancywort

5 (3) **a** Leaves **fleshy** (succulent) or **leathery,** hairless, closely crowded on stems (appearing spirally arranged). ━━━━━━▶ 6

    b Leaves on plant **not fleshy,** alternate. Leaves and plant generally bristly or downy. ━━━━━━━━━━▶ 7

6 (5) **a** Leaves 0.5–2 cm long, **very thick, waxy-green, oval, blunt, midrib obscure.** Plant 20–40 cm tall with several erect stems. **Exudes white milky juice** (when cut). Flowers **cup-shaped,** green in open umbel-like heads.

inflorescence

> *Euphorbia paralias*
> Sea Spurge

    b Similar to **a** but more slender. Leaves rather thinner and **leathery, broadest above middle, tips pointed, midrib prominent below.**

> *Euphorbia portlandica*
> Portland Spurge

7 (5) **a** Plant erect, up to 80 cm tall, **dotted with red-based bristles**. Root-leaves **strap-shaped**, stalked, up to 15 cm long. Stem-leaves shorter, stalkless. Flowers in **curved** cyme clusters, buds resembling bunches of grapes, flower corollas **bright blue**, funnel-shaped with unequal lobes.

> *Echium vulgare*
> Viper's Bugloss

b Plant erect, **greyish-downy**, 30–60 cm tall. **smelling of mice**. Root-leaves 10–25 cm long, stalked, **elliptical, pointed**. Upper leaves stalkless, **lanceolate**. Inflorescence a **forked** cyme, flower corollas up to 1 cm across, widely funnel-shaped, five-lobed, **dull purplish-red**.

> *Cynoglossum officinale*
> Hound's Tongue

8 (3) **a** Leaves with margins **entire**. ——————▶ 9
  b Leaves with margins **toothed**. Flowers nettle- or snapdragon-like.
  ——————————▶ 17

9 (8) **a** Plant **hairless**. ——————————▶ 10
  b Plant **hairy** (at least in part). ————————▶ 13

10 (9) **a** Plant prostrate to ascending, stems **four-angled**, up to 30 cm long. Leaves **oval, pointed**, stalkless **with black dots below**. Flowers solitary, on slender stalks in leaf-axils, corolla salmon-pink (sometimes blue or pink), **flat** and **wheel-shaped**.

flower

> *Anagallis arvensis*
> Scarlet Pimpernel

  b Plant with **distinct rosette** of leaves at base. ————▶ 11

11 (10) **a** Stem-leaves **oval triangular, joined in pairs** to form **rings round stem**. Rosette leaves broadest above middle. Plant erect, waxy-grey-green. Flowers in loose forking cymes, corollas six- to eight-lobed, yellow, 10–15 mm across.

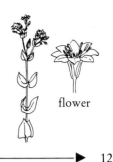

flower

> *Blackstonia perfoliata*
> Yellow-wort

    b Leaf arrangement **unlike that of a.** ⟶ 12

12 (11) **a** Stem leaves **oval-elliptical**. Rosette leaves broadest above middle. Plant erect, 10–40 cm tall. Flowers in more or less dense forking cymes on top of stem, corolla tube long, lobes **flat**, oval, **pink**.

flower

> *Centaurium erythraea*
> Common Centaury

    b Stem-leaves pointed, **oval-lanceolate**, 1–2 cm long. Rosette leaves **oblong**. Plant branched, 5–30 cm tall. Flowers, corolla tubes **purple**, four-to-five-lobed, **bell-shaped, calyx** of four or five **equal, narrow, erect** lobes.

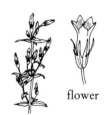

flower

> *Gentianella amarella*
> Autumn Gentian

    c Similar to **b** but differs mainly in its calyx in which two **wide-oval acute sepals overlap the two narrow-lanceolate inner ones**. Corollas **blue-lilac**. In the north of England and Scotland.

> *Gentianella campestris*
> Field Gentian

flower

13 (9) **a** Plant **low growing, mat-forming, far-creeping, faintly thyme-scented**. Leaves 4–8 mm long, **flat**. Flowers small, purplish, in dense heads on bluntly angled flower-stems, **very hairy on two opposite sides**.

stem section

> *Thymus drucei*
> Wild Thyme

    b Plant **without the combined features of a.** ⟶ 14

14 **(3) a** Plant **stickily hairy.** ──────────────▶ 15

   b Plant **hairy but not sticky.** ──────────────▶ 16

15 **(14) a** Plant erect, up to 45 cm tall. Leaves covered with **long** white hairs. Flowers in rather dense terminal heads, petals white, **notched for more than half their length.** Capsules 7–10 mm long, **curved.**

> *Cerastium glomeratum*
> Sticky Mouse-ear

b Plant 1–20 cm tall, branching at base. Stem-leaves **oval-oblong**, all with **short** white hairs. Petals white, **slightly notched.** Upper bracts and sepals **with broad silvery margins.** Capsules 4.5–6.5 mm long, **scarcely curved.**

sepal

> *Cerastium semidecandrum*
> Little Mouse-ear

c Plant creeping and ascending, 7–30 cm. Branching open. Resembles **b** but **without silvery margins** to the bracts and sepals. Petals **shorter than sepals,** white. Capsules 5–7.5 mm long, **straight.**

> *Cerastium atrovirens*
> Sea Mouse-ear

16 **(14) a** Plant **creeping and ascending,** up to 45 cm. Leaves **hairy,** dark green, **lanceolate,** broadest at base, stalkless. Flowers 3–12 mm across in loose cymes, petals white, **notched,** equal to or slightly longer than sepals, ten stamens.

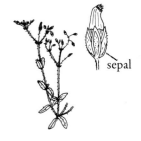

> *Cerastium holosteoides*
> Common Mouse-ear

b Plant **low spreading** to **bushy branched,** 1–25 cm tall. Leaves up to 6 mm long, **oval, pointed.** Petals white, **undivided,** shorter than sepals, Capsules **flask-shaped.**

capsule

> *Arenaria serpyllifolia*
> Thyme-leaved Sandwort

17 (8) **a** Leaves **oval**, blunt or sharp-toothed, leaf surface may be **wrinkled.** ────────────► 18

   b Leaves **lanceolate, pointed.** ──────────────► 19

18 (17) **a** Leaves oval, **blunt-toothed**, pointed, stalked, leaf surface **wrinkled**, 3–7 cm long. Plant downy, erect, tufted, 15–60 cm tall. Flowers in opposite pairs, corollas pale greenish-yellow, stamens red.

flower
leaf

> *Teucrium scorodonia*
> Woodsage

   b Leaves oval, hairless above, **sharp-toothed**, 6–12 mm long. Plant erect, 15–20 cm tall. Flower corolla, 5–7.5 mm long, two-lipped, lower lip longer than upper lip with purple streaks and yellow blotch.

leaf
flower

> *Euphrasia nemorosa*
> Common Eyebright

19 (17) **a** Leaves 1.5–4 cm long, stalkless, **few blunt** teeth. Plant erect, **very stickily hairy**, 10–50 cm tall. Flowers in long terminal racemes, calyx **tubular**, ribbed, with four spreading teeth, corollas bright yellow, lower three-lobed lip much longer than upper untoothed lip.

leaf

> *Parentucellia viscosa*
> Yellow Bartsia

   b Leaves stalkless, **narrowly lanceolate**. Plant erect, **more or less hairless**. Stem up to 50 cm tall, **black spotted**. Flowers in short leafy spikes, calyx **inflated and bladder-like** in fruit (**rattles**), corolla yellow, two-lipped, upper lip flattened on each side with two short violet teeth.

flower
leaf

> *Rhinanthus minor*
> Yellow Rattle

1   **a** Leaves **deeply lobed** or **pinnatifid.** ─────────────▶ 2

      b Leaves **compound.** ─────────────────────▶ 4

2 (1) **a** Leaves variable in shape. Basal and stem-leaves **pinnatifid.** Basal leaves with **large terminal lobes, all more or less cottony below.** Plant 30–100 cm tall with **furrowed stems.** Flower-heads in terminal umbel-like corymb, heads 15–25 mm across, ray florets bright yellow.

> *Senecio jacobaea*
> Ragwort

leaf

      b Leaves **rounded** in outline of five to seven lobes, widening at tips. ─▶ 3

3 (2) **a** Plant branched, spreading, with **long** (1–2 cm) **hairs** on stems. Flowers 3–7 mm across with five pink notched petals and ten **rosy-pink anthers.**

> *Geranium molle*
> Dove's-foot Crane's-bill

flower

leaf

capsule

      b As **a** but **closely downy, not hairy.** Petals 2–4 mm wide, dingy mauve, notched, five to ten stamens **lacking anthers.**

> *Geranium pusillum*
> Small-flowered Crane's-bill

4 (1) **a** Leaves **palmate** to base, leaflets further cut, bright green, sparsely hairy. Plant 10–40 cm tall. Stem and leaves often red-flushed. Flowers stalked, five-petalled, pink with orange or purple anthers.

> *Geranium robertianum*
> Herb-Robert

flower

leaf   capsule

      b Leaves **of other arrangement.** ──────────────▶ 5

5 (4) **a** Leaves **two- to three-pinnate**, base of leaves with **whitish pointed stipules**. Plant spreading, up to 30 cm, **usually stickily hairy**. Flowers one to nine in loose umbels, five-petalled, often unequal, rose–purple to white, often with **black spots** at base.

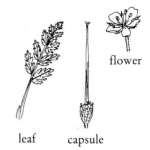

flower

leaf   capsule

> *Erodium cicutarium*
> Common Stork's Bill

b Leaves **one-pinnate**, may appear **trifoliate** with stipules at leaf bases.
───────────────────────────────▶ 6

6 (5) **a** Basal rosette leaves of seven to twelve pairs of leaflets. Leaflets **increasing in size upwards**, all with toothed margins. Stem-leaves similar but smaller, **smells of cucumbers when crushed**. Plant erect, 15–40 cm tall, branched stems terminate in globular heads of tiny greenish flowers.

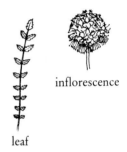

inflorescence

leaf

> *Poterium sanguisorba*
> Salad Burnet

b Leaves appear **trifoliate** with stipules at leaf bases. ─────────▶ 7

7 (6) **a** Leaflets **blunt oval**, blunt toothed, **all stickily hairy** (sand sticks to them). Plant **creeping and ascending**, 30–60 cm long, up to 30 cm tall. **Hairy all round**. Flowers 'pea-like', **pink**.

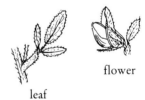

flower

leaf

> *Ononis repens*
> Restharrow

b Leaflet margins **entire**. Plant 10–50 cm **erect or sprawling**. Flower-stems up to 8 cm long, two to eight **yellow or orange** 'pea-like' flowers per head.

> *Lotus corniculatus*
> Bird's-foot-trefoil

Bibliography

Barnes, R.S.K. (1978). *The Coastline*. John Wiley, Chichester.

Chapman, V.J. (1978). *Coastal Vegetation* (2nd edn.). Pergamon, Oxford.

Clapham, A.R., Tutin, T.G. and Warburg, E.F. (1981). *Excursion Flora of the British Isles* (3rd edn.). Cambridge University Press, Cambridge.

Fitter, R., Fitter, A. and Farrer, A. (1984). *Guides to the Grasses, Sedges, Rushes and Ferns of Britain and Northern Europe*. Collins, London.

Haslam, S.M., Sinker, C.A. and Wolseley, P.A. (1975). British water plants. *Field Studies*, 4, pp. 243–351.

Hubbard, C.E. (1984). *Grasses* (3rd edn.). Penguin Books, London.

Jermy, A.C., Chater, A.O. and David, R.W. (1982). *Sedges of the British Isles*. Botanical Society of the British Isles.

Long, S.P. and Mason, C.F. (1983). *Saltmarsh Ecology*. Blackie,

McClintock, D. and Fitter, R.S.R. (1956). *Pocket Guide to Wild Flowers*. Collins, London.

Ranwell, D.S. (1972). *Ecology and Salt Marshes and Sand Dunes*. Chapman and Hall, London.

Rose, F. (1981). *The Wild Flower Key*. Frederick Warne, London.

Index